Good Deeds

Good Deeds

Over 200 Suggestions for Random Acts of Kindness to Brighten
the Lives of Family, Friends, and Complete Strangers

JAMES CHARLTON

AND

BARBARA BINSWANGER

ST. MARTIN'S PRESS • NEW YORK

Design by Janet Tingey

A Thomas Dunne Book

ISBN O-312-09899-5

First Edition: September 1993

10 9 8 7 6 5 4 3 2 1

With special thanks to Vilma Bergane, Debbie Binswanger, Lenore Binswanger, Anne Charlton, Tom Dunne, Jill Friedman, Lauren Friedman, Rose Heifetz, Ralph Kalish, Anne Lanigan, John Levinsohn, Blake Lochrie, Maria Robbins, Charlotte Schield, Jill Smolowe, and Pete Wolverton.
You all know what your good deeds were.

Foreword

 $\mathcal{T}$ H I N K about the last time you tried to change lanes on a busy road and how long you had to wait before somebody let you in. Do you remember the frustration you felt as you peered over your shoulder into the rush of oncoming traffic? Do you remember the feeling of gratitude and relief you felt when a driver finally slowed down and waved you over?

Or a time when you returned from a stay in the hospital or a long trip and a friend welcomed you with a cooked meal or flowers or some other expression of generosity?

Now picture a world where such simple acts of kindness and civility are commonplace, a place where generosity and thoughts are the norm and not the exception. It seems a far cry from the stressful demands of modern living that all too often grind down our good manners and spirits.

But that kinder and gentler world is still a noble goal, and one that is within our reach. We're not saying that you need to become another Mother Teresa. What we're talking about doesn't take a great deal of effort or require major changes in your personality. We are suggesting small gestures that can have a big impact.

Good Deeds offers a few ideas to brighten the lives of our families, friends, and even total strangers. There are hundreds of tried and true suggestions and advice included here. Some won't be right for you or won't apply to your town or family, but others are for everyone and just make good civic sense. And since we all know that what goes around comes around, your outlook will improve, too. The ripple effect is the operative principle.

You'll find that some of the suggestions are charitable in nature. But these are not big-ticket items requiring large expenditures (and are not meant to replace your usual philanthropic contributions). Rather they call for spending a few dollars here or there, or for making a donation of something that otherwise would have gone to waste.

Some of the ideas call for a bit of planning; for others, spontaneity is the key. Some are what were once considered common courtesies that sadly have become uncommon. And a few are reminders that occasionally the kindest act is to do or say nothing.

So make *Good Deeds* a habit. Keep it by your bed or in your desk drawer. You'll discover ways to apply the Golden Rule that your kindergarten teacher never thought to use.

Good Deeds

Feed a stranger's expired parking meter.

Pay the toll for the car behind you.

Give up your seat on the bus.

Spare someone's feelings.

If you have a full grocery cart, let someone with just a few items go ahead of you in the checkout line.

Hold the door for the person behind you.

Give directions to someone who is obviously lost but too embarrassed to ask for help.

Write a thank-you note when it is not necessary.

Give someone a compliment.

When you are driving, let a pedestrian cross in front of you.

Smile and say good morning to people you don't really know but see everyday on your way to work.

The next time someone asks you to do her a favor, do it.

Pick up litter, especially potentially dangerous litter like rusty nails or a broken bottle.

Let bygones be bygones.

Do an errand for an infirm neighbor.

Paint over some graffiti.

Send your child's teacher a thank-you note.

Call an old friend.

Tell your friend who's on a diet that she looks great.

Allow someone to save face.

Give your loose change to the next homeless person you see.

Resist the urge to send a chain letter to your six best friends.

Tell a white lie.

Volunteer to pick up a friend's relatives at the airport when they are arriving for a wedding or funeral.

Introduce yourself to a new neighbor.

Thank your mail carrier.

Turn the other cheek.

Volunteer an evening a week at the nearest hospital.

Tip generously.

Bring a meal to a family who has just lost a loved one.

Return something you've borrowed from a friend.

Adopt a stray animal.

Let your spouse win an argument.

Visit an elderly relative.

Send a wedding present to a couple you care about even if you weren't invited to the wedding.

Smile at a police officer.

Give a sucker an even break.

Don't expect favors to be returned.

Offer to buy stamps for a neighbor when you're going
to the post office.

Give your teenage baby-sitter the freebie cosmetic samples you got
with your department-store purchase.

Ask someone if he's lost weight.

Send a child a valentine or greeting card.

Have your old coats cleaned before you give them
to the Salvation Army.

Make polite small talk.

At a buffet, bring an older person a plate.

Put the toilet seat down.

Don't stop giving a relative a gift even if he doesn't say thank you.

Give batteries with gifts requiring them.

Phone a widower on his wife's birthday to share a special memory.

Surprise a teacher with a box of miscellaneous school supplies— she/he probably spends much of her/his own money making sure the children have enough pencils and scissors.

Save shirts with worn collars and frayed cuffs for art-class smocks.

Use your special skills and talents to teach a woodworking,
sewing, nutrition, study skills, volleyball, or cooking class
at a boy's or girl's club.

Buy at least one box of cookies from every Girl Scout who calls.

Be a walking/exercise buddy for your friend
who is trying to lose weight.

Invite a friend's family over for dinner when she is out of town
on a business trip.

Plan an extra spot or two at a holiday table and fill them
with people who would otherwise be alone.

Clear the table without being asked.

Forgive and forget.

Load the dishwasher even when it's not your turn.

Offer to drive a coworker to the office while her car is in the shop.

Bite your tongue.

Donate old toys and books to a child-care center, homeless
shelter, or children's hospital.

Send a note to a widow on her wedding anniversary
just to say you remember.

Give blood.

Take your old magazines to a retirement home.

Spend a few hours with a shut-in while their caregiver takes a walk, gets a haircut, or just takes a much needed break.

Sandwich criticism between two compliments.

Give a mom with a new baby a rest by taking the older children
to the park for a couple of hours.

Make the first move to patch up a quarrel.

Schedule time to read aloud to a group of children
or senior citizens.

Next time you're annoyed with your kids for acting so childishly, remember that they're children.

Sit with a friend in a hospital waiting room.

Display and/or use the gift your child or grandchild made for you.

Call a sick friend.

Let a sibling win a game.

Give a relative you don't like the benefit of the doubt.

Help a friend with his/her homework.

If your dining companion has something stuck
between her teeth, tell her.

Work a religious holiday for a friend of a different faith.

Offer to baby-sit instead of giving a baby present.

Let a driver who needs to change lanes cut in front of you.

Don't wait to be asked.

Take in a lost dog or cat and try to find the owner.

If you borrow ingredients from a neighbor for a recipe, return the item with some of what you have cooked.

Offer to pick up your neighbor's mail when he is on vacation.

Instead of a cut Christmas tree, buy a living Christmas tree and plant it after the holiday.

Collect and bring your hotel freebies (soap, shampoo, etc.)
to a homeless shelter.

When biking, give a warning shout to joggers when coming up
behind them.

Offer to bring your secretary coffee.

Drive a friend to a doctor's appointment.

Thank your bus driver.

Ask friends and family to make a donation to a favorite charity
in lieu of flowers for a funeral.

Break the ice.

Bring dinner to the home of someone who has just returned
from the hospital or had a baby.

Give the person in front of you the penny
she needs to make exact change.

Be your child's advocate; don't assume it's her fault.

Shovel your neighbor's walk.

Give someone a ride to the airport.

When you take food to a friend, put your name on the bottom of the container, or, better yet, put it in something that does not need to be returned.

Throw a neighbor's newspaper up on their porch.

If you can't say something nice, don't say anything at all.

If a friend or neighbor is returning home from an extended trip,
leave milk and orange juice in her refrigerator.

Give a sympathetic look to a mother struggling with
a screaming child.

If you notice a coworker's fly is open, tell him.

Even if you are with a group, leave room for people
to pass you on an escalator.

Take a widow or widower out to dinner.

If you're going away for the holidays, loan your car to a
(safe-driving) friend who has out-of-town guests.

Move over to the right lane when another driver wants to pass.

Don't make someone feel worse than she already feels.

Put a note with a poem, thought, or joke in your child's lunch box or backpack.

Make arrangements to donate leftover food from a wedding or other big event to a food bank or soup kitchen.

You've caught a foul ball at a baseball game.
Give it to the boy or girl sitting behind you.

Say hello to the next person of a different color you pass.

Give someone your undivided attention.

Refill and replace the ice tray.

Return your shopping cart.

Buy a child a tacky plastic present that her parents can't
(in good taste) let themselves buy her.

Do not give a child any present that makes such an irritatingly
loud or shrill noise that it is certain to drive her parents crazy.

Keep a secret.

Remember to tip the chambermaid at your hotel or motel.

Give up a disputed parking space.

Write a letter to a serviceperson overseas through
Operation Dear Abby.

Let a pregnant woman or parent with a small child use a public bathroom ahead of you.

Send a newspaper clipping of interest to a friend in another city.

When leaving a message on an answering machine, speak slowly enough so that the recipient can write down your phone number without having to replay the tape.

Leave the date and time of your call on
telephone answering machines.

Help someone struggling with a stroller up the stairs, onto an
escalator, or through a door.

When visiting, spend some time playing with or reading to your
host's small children.

Strip your bed and remake it with clean sheets after
an overnight stay at a friend's home.

Don't make promises you can't keep.

Reintroduce yourself when you greet someone you haven't seen
in a while and/or don't know very well.

Introduce yourself to an acquaintance's companion or spouse, if she doesn't do it for you; in all likelihood she has momentarily forgotten your name.

Order duplicates of photos to send to family members or friends and then remember to send them.

Replace the roll of toilet paper if you use the last piece.

Where it's the law, pick up after your dog. And, yes, there are people who pick up after other dogs as well.

Find a subtle way to tell a friend he's mispronouncing or misusing a word (if you think he'd like to know) such as "I'm never sure—is it Creesus or Croesuz."

Remember that for some people ignorance is bliss.

Save your practical jokes for people who appreciate them.

Be sensitive to your audience when it comes to humor, gossip, possessions, and politics.

When looking over your child's school project, comment only on the good parts; let her teacher handle the rest.

Don't overpraise.

Write a fan letter to an author.

Remind a discouraged friend or family member of past successes.

Take care of a neighbor's house plants when she's on vacation.

Give credit where credit is due.

Treat adolescents with respect; they will then often act
as though they deserve it.

Remember we're all in this together.

Keep aspirin in your desk, even if you don't use it, in case a coworker needs it.

If you are regularly asked for directions, keep a photocopy of a town street map to give to the next traveler who needs help.

Instead of sending flowers to the hospital, send them
to the home a week or so after the patient has been discharged
when he or she really needs a lift.

Offer to pick up and/or return library books for a shut-in.

When a relative or friend is in the hospital, clean their apartment
or home (or arrange to have it done) the day before discharge.

Bring your (well-behaved) pet to a nursing home
during visiting hours.

Take old paperbacks and playing cards to a senior citizen center.

Take old catalogs to a kindergarten class where they
can be recycled into collages.

Write a thank-you note to a legislator whose actions you approve.

Finish your conversation quickly if there are others waiting
for the pay phone you are using.

Wheel a neighbor's garbage can to the curb on pickup day.

Offer to change your seat on a plane or train,
if it allows a family to sit together.

Order a simple meal if you're out to dinner
with a friend who's dieting.

If you see a couple or group taking pictures of one another,
offer to take one of the whole group.

Write a complimentary letter to the supervisor of a clerk or service person who has been particularly helpful to you.

Take a deep breath and be polite to a telephone solicitor.

Be on time even if this means changing your habits and leaving fifteen minutes earlier than usual.

Call if you're going to be late.

Wipe out the bathtub after you use it.

Make someone feel important.

Resist the urge to give your slightly out-of-shape spouse a health-club membership for Christmas.

Don't assume that a friend who asks for an honest opinion really wants one.

Ask your dinner host for one of his or her recipes.

If a person ahead of you in the grocery or fast-food line (adult or child) is short of the cash needed to make his purchase, quietly signal the clerk that you'll make up the difference.

Have your car washed by the kids raising money for a class trip.

If you borrow a car, return it with a full tank of gas.

Tell your loved ones that they are loved.

Out of the blue you get an unwanted job offer. Recommend someone who you think might be interested.

You're burning the midnight oil at work and feel a gnawing in the pit of your stomach. Before you slip out to the deli to get a sandwich, see if another late-working colleague also wants something to eat.

Slip a note in the interoffice mail commending a colleague on a job well done.

Your mate must work late unexpectedly. Set the VCR to tape his/her favorite television show.

Put the toilet paper in the dispenser the way your spouse prefers. While you're at it, squeeze the toothpaste from the bottom.

Compliment a friend on a new haircut, pair of glasses, or beard. People are hypersensitive when it comes to all things facial.

Good friends call when things are rosy;
better friends call when times are blue.

For women only. Carry a tampon with you at all times;
sooner or later another woman will be grateful.

Give a jump start to someone whose car has a dead battery.

Help someone whose car is stuck in snow or mud
by giving the vehicle a push.

You have come across a lost toy in a shop, restaurant, or even on
the sidewalk. Give what is surely a beloved item to the store
manager or put it in a conspicuous place, so the distraught child
who dropped the treasure (or the equally distraught parent) has a
chance of finding it.

Ask permission of the parent before offering a child a sweet treat.

You're at the laundromat, staring at the dry clothes that are occupying the dryer you need. Resist the urge to dump them out in a heap. Give their tardy owner a nice surprise by having them neatly folded when he returns.

Clear your closets of unwanted wire clothes hangers
and give them to your dry cleaner.

Hold your tongue when the person ahead of you
in the grocery-store express line has eleven items instead of ten.

Stop to help someone whose overloaded bag
has spilled its contents.

Plant flowers or bulbs in your favorite park.

Organize (or be an active participant in) your neighborhood's crime watch or beautification association.

Suggest that your local supermarket set up a "food pantry" box where shoppers can leave donations for a local soup kitchen or other facility. And then make regular donations.

Organize an "old coat drive" through your place of worship,

your child's school, or another civic organization.

Then donate the coats to an organization

that will distribute them to those who need them.

Buy a brownie at a bake sale.

Send a contribution to a charity event, even if you can't attend.

Put your cellular phone to good use;
report a dangerous or erratic driver, a disabled vehicle,
or an accident to the police or state troopers.

Plan a celebration for a friend or family member for an event that
would not ordinarily call for one.

Assemble a "this is your life" photo album for a friend or family member's milestone birthday.

Take someone else's child out for a special event or treat.

Make a higher bid than necessary at a fund-raising auction.

Acknowledge with a thank you the small services that strangers perform for you every day.

Pay more than the suggested admission price when you visit a museum.

Acknowledge a homeless person with a hello and a smile.

Sometimes children waiting in line are overlooked

at busy shops and restaurant counters.

Help a child get the attention of a sales clerk or service person.

Go through your cupboards and give all the still-good,

but unlikely-to-ever-be-eaten canned goods and staples

to a food bank.

Stop smoking.

Organize a family reunion and invite some estranged relatives.

Support a local artist.

Spend part of Thanksgiving or Christmas day working in a soup kitchen or homeless shelter.

Make a list of your favorite local shops and services and give it to a new neighbor.

Pay the bus or subway fare for the next person in line.

Make a donation to every child who
"trick or treats" for UNICEF.

When you're ordering a take-out sandwich and you know
it's going to be more than you can eat, ask the clerk to wrap the
two halves separately. Then give the other half to the next
homeless person you see.

Offer to help a technophobic friend install a new piece of
electronic equipment.

Surprise your new neighbors on their moving-in day by having
pizzas delivered for their dinner.

A friend who has just been fired probably feels like a social pariah.
Invite him or her out to lunch—on you.

R.S.V.P. to every invitation, no matter how casual the event.

When you're visiting friends for the weekend, bring them a gift. Something for their home, the makings of a meal, a few bottles for the liquor cabinet. If you accompany your hosts to the grocery store, consider making a contribution at the checkout line.

Make an effort to change a habit that drives
your family or friends crazy.
No more "That's just the way I am" excuses.

Buy books.

Support your local library. See if they can use your old books for
their shelves or for a fund-raising book sale.

Read aloud to your children. They will love it, even if they have already learned to read.

Let someone off the hook.

Become a literacy volunteer.

Admire an ugly baby. Say to the parent, "You must be having a lot of fun with her" or "He seems very alert."

You're at a self-service gas station and notice someone struggling with the pump. Offer a helping hand.

A friend is moving to a different city. Send her a subscription to her new home town's city magazine.

Resist the urge to pat the stomach of a pregnant woman.

Always make sure that someone in your family knows where you can be reached when you're away from home.

Do something just to please your parents.

Do something just to please your spouse.

It is cold. You see a mother with a toddler who is not wearing a hat or mittens. Give that mom a break; don't inform her that her child really should be wearing a hat and mittens.

Let someone down easy.

Notify catalog companies of duplicate mailings.

Take away the car keys or call a cab. Do anything you have to, but don't let a friend or family member drive drunk.

Drive less—ride a bike, walk, or take public transportation.

Turn off the water while you're brushing your teeth.

Take shorter showers.

Use a sponge rather than a paper towel.

Turn off the lights when you leave the room.

Whether it is a school board election, local referendum, or Presidential election, vote. Even if it is an expected landslide, don't give up your right to vote.

Become a "surrogate" grandparent for the children of young neighbors or friends.

Offer your services as a backup baby-sitter if a friend's usual arrangements break down.

Bring home flowers for your spouse for absolutely no reason.

Your teenager is sick and can't deliver the newspapers or work her part-time job. If the timing doesn't conflict with your work, fill in for her.

After the wedding, send the flower arrangements to a nursing
home or hospital.

Leave places cleaner than you found them.

Phone home.

If you have your own good deeds to suggest for the next edition
please send a postcard to us at:

Good Deeds
St. Martin's Press
175 Fifth Avenue
New York, N.Y. 10010